Chestnut Farm

1860

Geoffrey Patterson

ANDRE DEUTSCH

First published 1980 by
André Deutsch Limited
105 Great Russell Street London WC1

Copyright © 1980 by Geoffrey Patterson
All rights reserved

Printed in Great Britain by
Ebenezer Baylis & Son Ltd Worcester

British Library Cataloguing in Publication Data
Patterson, Geoffrey
    Chestnut farm, 1860.
    1. Agriculture – Great Britain – History –
    19th century – Juvenile literature
    I. Title
    630´.941   S455

ISBN 0 233 97208 0

First published in the United States of America 1980
Library of Congress Number 79-86-46

This is the story of the Finbow family, and the farm they lived on over a hundred years ago. They called their farm Chestnut Farm, and Edward Finbow lived there with his wife, Mary, his daughter, Ruth and his two sons, Harry and George.

Farms were smaller in those days, but most of the work had to be done by hand. So Farmer Finbow and his family all worked very hard to make a living.

The most important animals on the farm were the two
beautiful heavy horses. They did all the work that tractors do
today. Harry and George made sure that they were well

looked after. Mary and Ruth cared for the chickens and
geese. They had little money to buy food, so Mary was pleased
when Edward managed to catch a rabbit for supper.

In the winter Edward moved the cows from the fields to the shelter of the farmyard, so he could keep them warm and dry. He spread straw on the ground for them. Each day he fed them with hay and mangolds (mangolds look like turnips and cows love them). Edward cut the mangolds, which had been specially grown for winter feeding, in a machine called a root cutter. The hay was grown during the summer and stored in stacks.

Every day the cows had to be milked by hand, first thing in the morning and in the afternoon. Each cow took about fifteen minutes to milk and although it was hard work it was warm sitting close to the cow.

Joe Rumsey, who lived in a cottage down the lane, and other villagers came to the farm to buy milk. Ruth filled the jug out of a pail.

The family used all the milk that was left to make cheese and butter. Mary sold the cheese in the town on market day.

By spring the wind had dried out the land and the grass had begun to grow again. So Harry moved the cows from the yard back to the meadow to graze.

Harry and George forked the muck made by the cows during the winter on to a tip-up cart called a 'tumbril'. They spread the muck on the fields in heaps to be ploughed in later. It was smelly work.

"That should make the corn grow," said George as Harry piled the last fork load on to the cart.

When the land was dry enough, it was ploughed. George was up very early in the morning to feed the horses and harness them to the plough. By six o'clock they were ready to start work.

Up and down they went turning the soil over in neat furrows. By three o'clock both George and the horses had had enough. Between them they had ploughed an acre of land.

Ploughing a field in straight lines is very difficult. George was good at it, and he had won many prizes in village competitions.

As the plough turned over the earth, stones were thrown up. So before the seed could be sown, Edward paid the boys and girls of the village to pick them up and throw them into the tumbril. Harry took the stones away to fill in the ruts in the cart tracks around the farm.

Then the soil was broken up into smaller pieces by using a

'harrow'. A harrow was a large rake with lots of spikes. George harnessed the horses again for this job. Now the fields were ready

for sowing. Edward kept some fields for rootcrops and others for wheat.

Edward scattered the seed corn by hand. This was called 'broadcasting'. He carried the seed in a tray slung around his neck and cast it out with both hands as he walked across the field.

As soon as the sowing was finished, flocks of hungry birds settled on the earth to eat the grain. Children from the village were employed to scare them off with wooden rattles called 'clappers'.

Every Friday Ruth baked the bread for the coming week. She heated the oven with bundles of sticks called 'faggots'. When it was hot enough she raked out the ashes and put in the dough.

Mary made the butter in the cool dairy. She poured the cream

from the milk into a 'butter churn', a barrel with a handle to turn
it over and over. After a while the cream thickened and turned into
butter. Then Mary added salt and sometimes marigold petals to
give it some colour.

Edward and his sons kept their eyes on the wheat all through the summer as the sun and the rain made it grow.

One day in July Edward and Harry stood by the gate and wondered if it would stay fine. The wheat looked good, and they could hear the wind whistling through it. Edward decided it was time to cut it. He needed all the help he could get from the village to gather in the harvest.

The wheat was cut with a scythe, a long pole with a curved blade at one end. The blade was kept sharp by rubbing a special stone across it. Each man kept his stone in his belt.

Harry was in charge of the men as they moved across the field swishing their scythes and cutting the wheat before

them. As it fell to the ground, Edward and the others gathered it up in armfuls to make sheaves. They tied the sheaves together in big bundles . . .

. . . six or eight of these sheaves would be set up against each other to make a 'stook'. The grain in the stooks soon ripened off and dried in the sun and wind.

Getting the harvest in was hungry work. Mary and the other wives brought baskets of bread and cheese and

sometimes meat wrapped in a moist cloth for the workers.
Mary also brought them a special brew of harvest beer in
a stone and wicker bottle.

When the stooks were dry they were loaded on the wagons and brought into the yard to be made into corn stacks.

First, branches and sharp briars were laid on the ground to prevent rats and mice from getting into the stack. Then the sheaves were piled carefully on top of each other, the ears of wheat pointing inwards, again to protect them from vermin. When the stack was high enough, it was thatched, to protect the sheaves from wind and rain.

When the last sheaf had left the field the women and children of the village came to 'glean', the name given to the practice of collecting the fallen ears of wheat. In good years they found enough to grind into bread flour for the winter. In a bad year there would at least be enough to feed the hens.

To thank everyone who had worked so hard getting the harvest
in, Edward arranged a special Harvest Supper. He paid for
everything even if there had been a poor harvest. The workers

made the most of this and really enjoyed themselves eating and drinking. After supper songs were sung and everyone felt a little sad that the harvest was over for another year.

In October, when things were not quite so busy, Edward decided it would be a good time to thresh the wheat. This was done to separate the grain from the straw. Edward hired a man to do this job who went from farm to farm with his traction engine and a threshing machine.

The traction engine drove the threshing machine by a long belt. The sheaves of wheat went in at the top of the machine, and grain came out of one end into sacks. The straw came out of the other. The straw was used in the winter for bedding.

When the threshing was over Edward, Harry and George went to Mr Fox the miller to sell the grain. Edward paid Mr Fox for his work in flour rather than money. The amount they agreed was 4lb from every sack of flour.

1860 was a good year with plenty of hay and straw to see the animals through the winter, but not every year was like this. Some years were hard and hungry ones.